BRITISH CLAS

ARRANGED FOR INTERMEDIATE PIANO SOLO

CHESTER MUSIC
(A division of Music Sales Limited)
8/9 Frith Street, London W1V 5TZ

This book © Copyright 1998 Chester Music Limited.
Order No. CH61428   ISBN 0-7119-6850-0

Music processed by Allegro Reproductions.
Cover design by Chloë Alexander.
Printed in Great Britain by Printwise (Haverhill) Limited, Haverhill, Suffolk.

CONTENTS

EARLY ONE MORNING

This simple melody has become one of the best-known traditional English folk tunes.

ANONYMOUS
Arr. Stephen Duro

Andante con moto

GREENSLEEVES

The true origins of this folk tune are uncertain,
but some believe it was written by Henry VIII.

HENRY VIII (ANON)
Arr. Stephen Duro

NOW IS THE MONTH OF MAYING

Morley wrote over 100 madrigals; this is one of his most popular.

THOMAS MORLEY
Arr. Stephen Duro

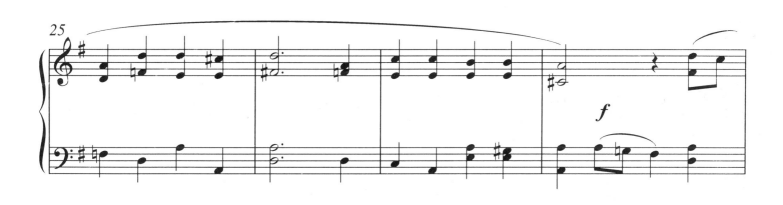

WHEN I AM LAID IN EARTH

from Dido And Aeneas

This tragic opera was written for a Chelsea girls' school.
'When I Am Laid In Earth' is the final moving lament.

HENRY PURCELL
Arr. Stephen Duro

Lento

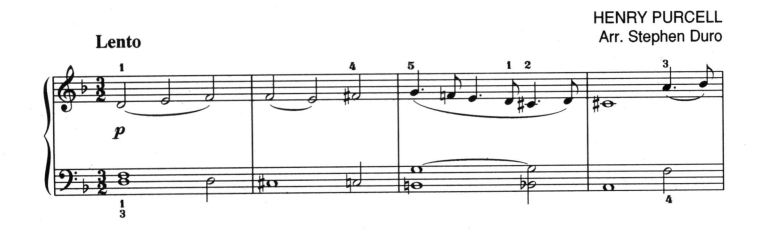

RONDO
from Abdelazer

As a theatre work Abdelazer was not a success,
but it contains some of Purcell's finest orchestral music.

HENRY PURCELL
Arr. Stephen Duro

HORNPIPE
from Water Music Suite in D

Handel spent much of his working life in England; the Water Music
was written for a royal pleasure trip down the Thames for George I.

GEORGE FREDERIC HANDEL
Arr. Stephen Duro

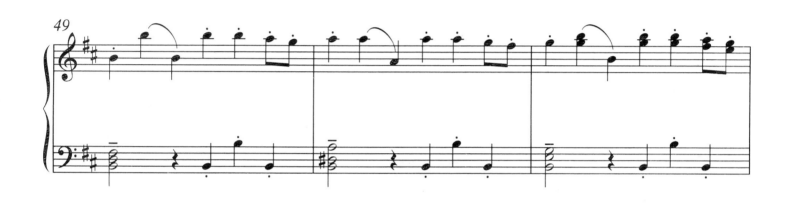

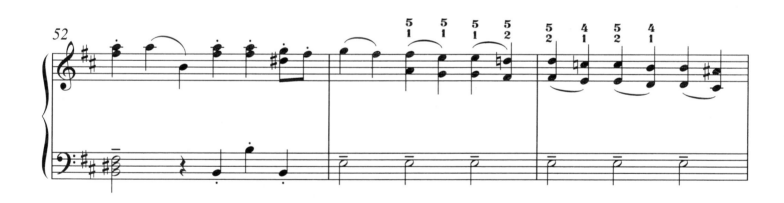

D.C. al Fine

RULE BRITANNIA

Originally written as part of the masque Alfred, Rule Britannia
has become an integral part of the Last Night of the Proms.

THOMAS ARNE
Arr. Stephen Duro

TRUMPET VOLUNTARY

For a long time this was thought to be by Purcell, but is
now known to be 'The Prince of Denmark's March' by Clarke.

JEREMIAH CLARKE
Arr. Stephen Duro

ARRIVAL OF THE QUEEN OF SHEBA

from Solomon

This is the Overture to Act III of the oratorio Solomon. The music actually
portrays the preparations for (rather than the arrival of) the Royal guest.

Allegro giocoso

GEORGE FREDERIC HANDEL
Arr. Stephen Duro

GAVOT

from Symphony No. 4 in F

This is from Boyce's 'Eight Symphonies in Eight Parts' (1760),
which were actually written as Overtures for various theatrical works.

WILLIAM BOYCE
Arr. Stephen Duro

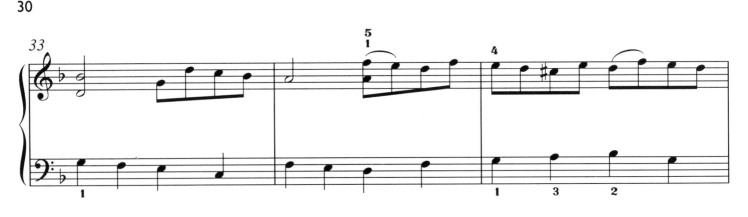

ONWARD CHRISTIAN SOLDIERS

Although best known for his collaboration with W.S. Gilbert,
Sullivan also worked as an organist, teacher and song and hymn tune writer.

ARTHUR SULLIVAN
Arr. Stephen Duro

THE SUN, WHOSE RAYS ARE ALL ABLAZE

from The Mikado

The Mikado is one of the best-known of Gilbert and Sullivan's collaborations.

ARTHUR SULLIVAN
Arr. Stephen Duro

Andante comodo

INTRODUCTION AND ALLEGRO, Op. 47

Theme

As with many of Elgar's works, this piece reflects the
inspiration of the Malvern Hills in Worcestershire.

EDWARD ELGAR
Arr. Stephen Duro

JUPITER FROM THE PLANETS

Theme

Of Holst's relatively small and varied output,
The Planets is undoubtedly his best known work.

GUSTAV HOLST
Arr. Stephen Duro

Andante maestoso

JERUSALEM

This rousing setting has become so popular it is now regarded as
a national anthem, and is the work for which Parry is best remembered.

HUBERT PARRY
Arr. Stephen Duro

FOLK SONGS FROM SOMERSET

from English Folk Song Suite

Vaughan Williams drew on English folk song as a source of inspiration for
many of his works. This suite was written for military band in 1923.

RALPH VAUGHAN WILLIAMS
Arr. Stephen Duro

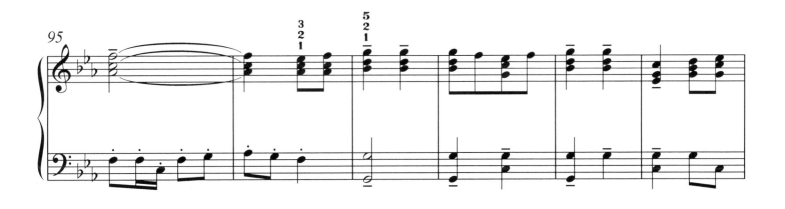

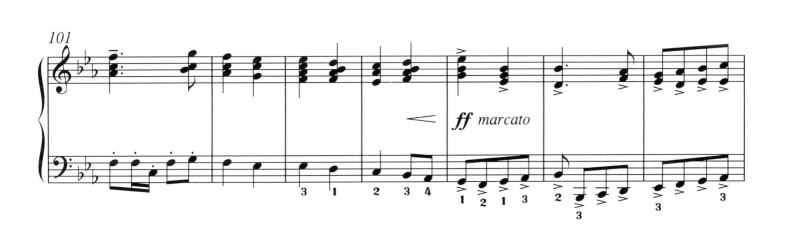

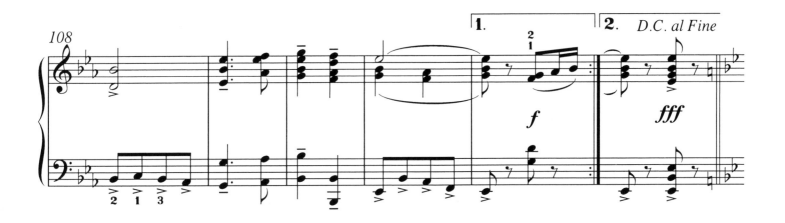

POMP AND CIRCUMSTANCE MARCH No. 1

Theme

This trio from March No. 1 contains the tune to which is sung
'Land Of Hope And Glory', evoking all the glory of the British Empire.

EDWARD ELGAR
Arr. Stephen Duro

CAVATINA
from The Deer Hunter

This beautifully simple tune has become popular through
its use in the film The Deer Hunter.

STANLEY MYERS/JOHN WILLIAMS
Arr. Stephen Duro

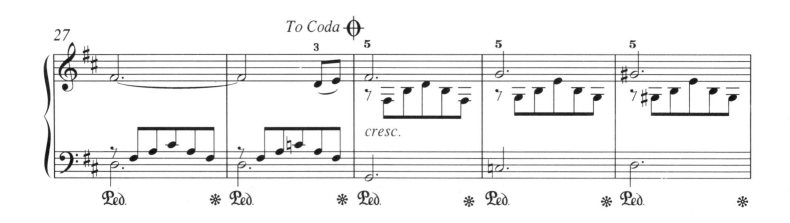

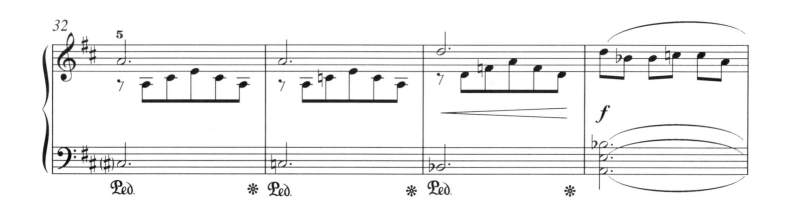

THE LAMB

This setting of the words from Blake's Songs of Innocence
is one of Tavener's most frequently performed works.

JOHN TAVENER
Arr. Stephen Duro

With extreme tenderness - flexible   **(moving forward)**

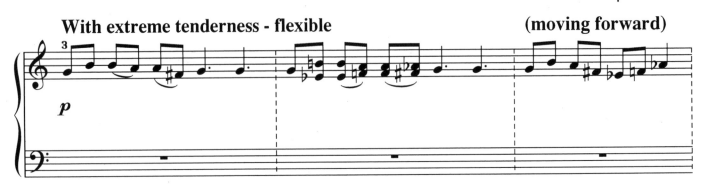

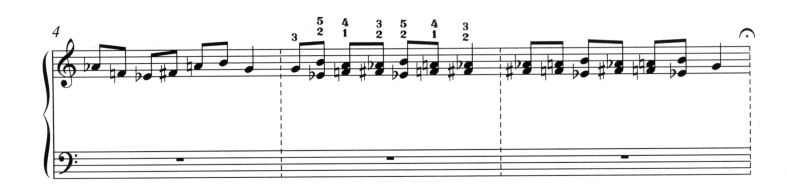

Poco meno mosso

A tempo - moving forward

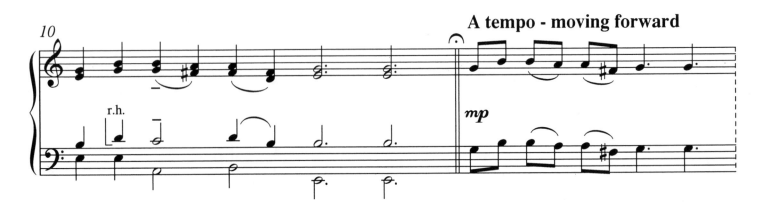

THE HEART ASKS PLEASURE FIRST

(The Promise/The Sacrifice)

Written for the film The Piano by Jane Campion, this music is described by one of
the characters as 'like a mood that passes through you... a sound that creeps into you'.

MICHAEL NYMAN

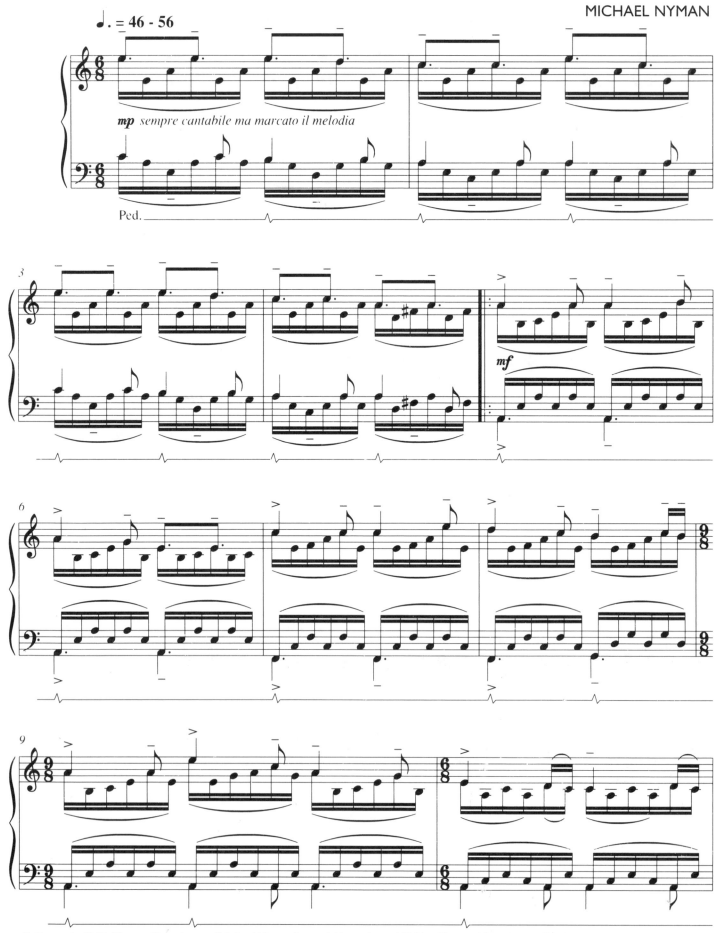

PIANO MUSIC
AVAILABLE FROM CHESTER MUSIC

CONTEMPORARY CLASSICS
Three collections of masterpieces of the 20th century superbly
arranged for intermediate piano solo. Including works by
Elgar, Ellington, Holst, Sibelius and Stravinsky.
Piano Solo 1 CH61181
Piano Solo 2 CH61182
Piano Duet CH61183

THE GREATEST CLASSICAL MOVIE ALBUM CH61387
Classical masterpieces of the cinema arranged for piano solo:
from *Four Weddings And A Funeral* to *Silence Of The Lambs*.

MANUEL DE FALLA PIANO ALBUM CH61279
Falla's best-known works arranged for intermediate piano solo.
Including works from *El Amor Brujo* and *The Three-Cornered Hat*.

MICHAEL NYMAN
FILM MUSIC FOR SOLO PIANO CH61400
A selection of pieces and arrangements by the composer of his
best-known film music. Including music from *The Draughtsman's
Contract, Drowning By Numbers, Carrington* and *The Piano*.

THE PIANO (Michael Nyman) CH60871
Original compositions for solo piano from the award-winning
film by Jane Campion.

REVISITING THE PIANO (Michael Nyman) CH61411
Four new arrangements available for the first time for solo piano,
plus the two favourite themes from the soundtrack of *The Piano*.

TUNES YOU'VE ALWAYS WANTED TO PLAY CH55834
MORE TUNES YOU'VE ALWAYS WANTED TO PLAY CH58750
DUETS YOU'VE ALWAYS WANTED TO PLAY CH61185
Bumper albums containing classical and traditional favourites
in excellent arrangements for intermediate pianists.

Chester Music
(A division of Music Sales Limited)
Exclusive distributors:
Music Sales Limited, Newmarket Road, Bury St Edmunds, Suffolk IP33 3YB.